Teaching Children the Value of Positive Thinking

by W. A. R. Boyer, Ph.D.
and Barb Rumson

Fearon Teacher Aids
A Division of Frank Schaffer Publications, Inc.

Body Illustrations: Steve Sullivan
Cover Illustration: Jeanette Courtin

Editors: Cindy Barden, Hanna Otero, Christine Hood
Book Design: Riley Wilkinson
Graphic Artists: Carol Arriola, Drew R. Moore

Fearon Teacher Aids products were formerly manufactured and distributed by American Teaching Aids, Inc., a subsidiary of Silver Burdett Ginn, and are now manufactured and distributed by Frank Schaffer Publications, Inc. FEARON, FEARON TEACHER AIDS, and the FEARON balloon logo are marks used under license from Simon & Schuster, Inc.

FE11027 — Developing Optimism Grades 2–3
© **Fearon Teacher Aids**
A Division of Frank Schaffer Publications, Inc.
23740 Hawthorne Boulevard
Torrance, CA 90505-5927

All rights reserved—Printed in the United States of America.
Copyright © 2000 Fearon Teacher Aids

Notice! Copies of student pages may be reproduced by the classroom teacher for classroom use only, not for commercial resale. No part of this publication may be reproduced for storage in a retrieval system, or transmitted in any form or by any means—electronic, mechanical, recording, etc.—without the written permission of the publisher. Reproduction of these materials for an entire school or school system is strictly prohibited.

Table of Contents

A Rule for Life 4

Introduction 5

Lesson 1
Discovering 6-9
Discussion Questions 9
Oliver and Pete at the Olympics 10-11
Friends 12
Cross-Curricular Extension Activities 13-14

Lesson 2
Communicating 15-17
Discussion Questions 17
Silent Communication 18
Shouting 19
Extension Activities 20
American Manual Alphabet 21
Morse Code and Other Common Codes 22

Lesson 3
Success Words 23-24
Cross Out the Negatives 25
Success Words 26
Phrases That Will Make You a Winner 27
Extension Activities 28-29

Lesson 4
Probe-Em 30-32
Probe-Em Scenarios 33
Extension Activities 34

Lesson 5
Believing Tower 35-36
Discussion Questions 36
I Believe I Can 37
Extension Activities 38-39

Lesson 6
On Your Mark, Get Set, Plan! 40-42
Extension Activities 43

Lesson 7
Smiles and Giggles 44-46
Smiles, Giggles, and Jokes 47
Extension Activities 48

Lesson 8
A Positive Attitude Is Contagious 49-50
Do I Have a Positive Attitude? 51
Extension Activities 52

Lesson 9
Rainbow Optimism 53-54
Extension Activities 55-56

Lesson 10
Smiles Are Contagious 57-58
Extension Activities 59
The Case of the Missing Smile 60

Lesson 11
The Optimists Club 61-62
Optimists Club Pledge 63
Optimists Club Membership Certificate 64

A Rule for Life
by John Wesley

Do all the good you can,

By all the means you can,

In all the ways you can,

In all the places you can,

At all the times you can,

To all the people you can,

As long as ever you can.

Introduction

Our society is constantly faced with innovation, change, and challenge. To cope positively with the unexpected, children should be prepared to identify, create, and embrace opportunities for learning and fulfillment. To do this, they need self-confidence and an optimistic point of view.

When faced with challenges, children, like adults, may need help to combat apprehension, self-doubt, and rigidity, which could result in stagnation and personal defeat.

Developing Optimism presents eleven complete lesson plans to help you provide a framework for children to develop a positive attitude toward life. Each unit includes a detailed, motivating presentation with objectives, a materials list, and an approximation of the time needed for each part of the lesson. You'll also find handouts, patterns, discussion questions, and student reproducibles. You can print the insights listed for each lesson on brightly-colored posterboard and add more of your own. Use these to decorate your classroom and as introductions to each lesson.

Following each lesson are easy-to-use cross-curricular extension activities. These art, music, science, math, social studies, and language arts ideas will help you extend and reinforce concepts learned in each lesson. A list of related reading material is also included.

As you join children in songs, stories, role-play, and more, you will encourage them to develop self-confidence and find ways to take an optimistic approach to life.

Developing Optimism will change your classroom dynamics by shifting the focus from negative to positive, from pessimistic to optimistic. As the title of Lesson 10 implies, you and your students will laugh a lot as you learn that a sunny disposition is wonderfully contagious.

Lesson 1

Discovering

Materials

copy of "Oliver and Pete at the Olympics" (pages 10–11)

copy of "Friends" (page 12)

2 two-inch (5-cm) white paper circles for each student

glue or tape

2 craft sticks per student

crayons or markers

additional materials for selected activities

Insights: Curiosity brings discovery. To learn, you must want to know.

Objective: Students will explore the difference between optimism and pessimism.

Time: Approximately 35–40 minutes
(Additional time may be needed depending on extension activities selected.)

Cut two circles per student from white construction paper, or make a pattern from light cardboard. Students can trace the patterns and cut their own circles.

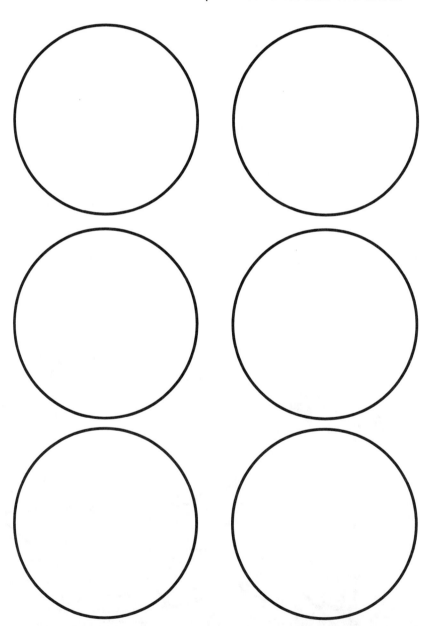

© Fearon Teacher Aids FE11027   reproducible

Discovering

Lesson 1

Time	Activity	Procedure
5 minutes	Introduction	*Begin with this chant:* First comes want, Then comes do, Then comes success for you. *Repeat with students several times.* **Teacher:** What makes someone a friend? *Pause for student responses.* **Teacher:** Think about why you like your best friend and how that person became your best friend. What qualities do you like best about that person? *Help students brainstorm words that describe their friends. Write their ideas on the chalkboard. Encourage students to include these traits: happy, sharing, caring, encouraging, helpful, kind, considerate, good (positive) attitude.* *Write the word* OPTIMIST *at the top of this list of positive qualities. Explain that an optimist is a person who has a cheerful outlook on life.* **Teacher:** No one is happy all the time. An optimist looks for ways to be happy and share that happiness with others. *Ask students if they know anyone who is grumpy, grouchy, or who complains most of the time. Ask for words that describe this type of person. Write their ideas on the chalkboard.* *At the top of this list, write the word* PESSIMIST. *Explain that a pessimist is a person who has a negative outlook on life. A pessimist fails to see happiness because he or she is always expecting something bad to happen.* **Teacher:** Have you ever read any stories or seen any movies about Winnie-the-Pooh and his friends? Do you think Eeyore, the donkey, is an optimist or a pessimist?

© Fearon Teacher Aids FE11027

Lesson 1

Discovering

Time	Activity	Procedure
	Introduction (continued)	Make a gloomy Eeyore face and wait for students to respond that Eeyore is a pessimist. Ask for some specific examples.
		Reassure students that most people are sad, or grumpy, or grouchy once in a while. That doesn't make a person a pessimist. A pessimist is a person who is sad or grumpy most of the time.
		Have students read the words optimist and pessimist.
		Teacher: Who would you rather have for a friend, an optimist or a pessimist?
		Today we are going to read a story about Oliver and Pete. Before we start, let's make optimistic and pessimistic faces to use as we listen.
10 minutes	Prepare Props	Give each child two crafts sticks, two 2-inch white paper circles, crayons, and markers.
		Ask students to draw two faces. One face should be optimistic. The other face should be pessimistic.
		When faces are finished, have students tape or glue them to the craft sticks.
10 minutes	Read Story	Read the story "Oliver and Pete at the Olympics." Ask students to listen to the story. Tell them that when you pause, they should hold up one of the faces to show what attitude the children in the story have at that time.
	Option	You may prefer to read the story once while students listen without responding. Read it a second time and have them participate as indicated above.
10 minutes	Discussion	Use the questions on the next page for group discussion after reading the story.

© Fearon Teacher Aids FE11027

Discovering

Lesson 1

Time	Activity	Procedure
5 minutes	Anchoring	**Teacher:** Let's review what we learned in the story. *Display the page "Friends." Read it together with students.* **Teacher:** Hold up your optimistic faces and shake them in the air if you agree. *Write these phrases on the chalkboard or chart paper as you say them. When you finish, have students chant them with you several times. Make it a fun, enthusiastic chant!* **Teacher:** I can be cheerful. I can be caring. I can be sharing. I can help others. I can encourage others. I can compliment others. I can have a positive attitude. I can be a friend.

Discussion Questions

1. Why was it important for everyone to listen to the principal's instructions?
2. How did most of the children feel about Olympic Day?
3. How did Pete feel about Olympic Day?
4. How did Pete show he had a pessimistic attitude? Give examples from the story.
5. How did Oliver show he was Pete's friend? Give examples from the story.
6. What happened when Pete joined the Olympics?
7. Could Pete and Oliver have fun at the Olympics even if they didn't win?
8. What is more important, winning an event or having fun trying? Why?
9. How do we know Pete appreciated what Oliver did for him?
10. Is Oliver the kind of person you would like to have for a friend? Why or why not?

© Fearon Teacher Aids FE11027

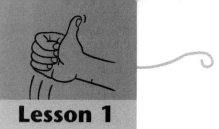

Lesson 1

Discovering

Oliver and Pete at the Olympics

The children sat in the assembly hall, wiggling with excitement. They knew the principal had some exciting news for them. They couldn't wait to hear what it was.

"Today is Olympics Day," the principal announced. "We are having our very own school Olympics competition."

That was great news! The Olympics were games. Everyone liked games. They listened as the principal explained the different events. Almost everyone smiled. They were looking forward to Olympic Day.
(Pause. The first time, remind students to respond by holding up their craft sticks with the optimistic or pessimistic faces.)

Pete and Oliver sat in the back row. Pete wasn't paying attention to the principal. Oliver turned to his friend and whispered, "Hey, this is going to be fun. Maybe you and I can win some medals, just like they do in the real Olympics. We're great!" ***(Pause)***

"Big deal," replied Pete. "Who cares about some dumb old games?" ***(Pause)***

When the principal finished talking, Oliver tugged on Pete's sleeve. "Come on, Pete," said Oliver. "It's time to get our gym clothes on so we'll be ready for the Olympics."

"Forget it," answered Pete. "It won't be fun anyway. I'm going to go play by myself." ***(Pause)***

"Wait. You'll see. We'll have a great time," said Oliver. ***(Pause)***

"We probably won't win anything. Why don't we go off and play together instead? No one will miss us," said Pete as he turned to walk away. ***(Pause)***

"No," said Oliver. "I'm going to join the Olympics and you should, too." ***(Pause)***

"If you do, you won't be my friend anymore," Pete said. ***(Pause)***

"I'm your friend, Pete, but I want to join the Olympics," insisted Oliver.

"I'm not playing any of those silly games," Pete said in a grumpy voice. ***(Pause)***

Oliver took Pete's arm and tugged at him until they got to the locker room. Reluctantly, Pete began changing into his gym clothes. "Hurry, Pete," said Oliver. "I'm ready."

"Forget it," grumbled Pete. "I have a knot in my dumb shoe. I can't get it out." Pete threw his shoe. It bounced off a locker and landed by Oliver. ***(Pause)***

Discovering

Lesson 1

Oliver picked up the shoe, untied the knot, and handed it back to Pete. "Get your shoe on and we'll get in line for the jumping contest. I bet we can win lots of medals. We're good jumpers," said Oliver. ***(Pause)***

Pete put his shoe on. "No way. I'll probably trip and fall." ***(Pause)***

"Stop being so pessimistic. You go ahead of me. I know you can jump really far," said Oliver as they joined the end of the line for the jumping contest. ***(Pause)***

When it was Pete's turn, he made a great jump. Everyone clapped. It was the longest jump so far. Pete looked surprised when he saw how far he had jumped. He turned back to Oliver and smiled. Then Oliver jumped. He had a great jump, too. He landed at exactly the same place as Pete had. They had tied for first place!

"Come on, let's try the next event. It's a race all the way around the track. We're great runners. Maybe we can win another prize," said Oliver. ***(Pause)***

"Forget it," said Pete. "That was just a lucky jump." ***(Pause)***

"No, it was a good jump and we can run a good race, too, if we try," said Oliver. ***(Pause)***

"All right, all right. Quit bugging me and I'll give it a try, but don't expect anything." ***(Pause)***

Oliver and Pete lined up with the other children at the starting line for the race. "On your mark . . . get set . . . GO!" shouted Coach Jenkins. The racers took off. At first Oliver and Pete were in the middle of the group. At least half the kids were ahead of them.

"Come on, Pete, we've got to try harder," shouted Oliver as he put on a burst of speed. ***(Pause)***

"Wait for me, Oliver. I'm not letting you get ahead of me," answered Pete. As the racers neared the finish line, everyone was getting tired and sweaty. Oliver looked at Pete, who was racing by his side. He gave his friend a big grin. They both gave a little more effort. Suddenly, they crossed the finish line side by side, right behind Jesse, the best runner in the whole school.

"We did it!" shouted Oliver. "We took second place! All right!" ***(Pause)***

"Second place? Really? Wow!" shouted Pete in surprise. ***(Pause)***

As Oliver and Pete waited with the other winners to get their ribbons, Pete said. "I didn't want to join the Olympics today, but you talked me into it. I didn't think it would be any fun, but I was wrong. It was fun. And best of all, we both won ribbons." ***(Pause)***

"Thanks for talking me into joining, Oliver. You really are a great friend."

The End

reproducible © Fearon Teacher Aids FE11027

Lesson 1

Friends

Friends care.

Friends share.

Friends are happy.

Friends help one another.

Friends encourage each other.

Friends have positive attitudes.

Discovering Extension Activities

Lesson 1

Art
- Have students draw pictures of themselves and friends doing something together. Below their pictures, ask students to write one or two sentences about their friends.
- Have students cut out cloud shapes from white construction paper and write words about the characteristics of optimists. Decorate the clouds by gluing white, fluffy cotton to the edges. Let students add glitter or other decorations. Use the clouds as part of a bulletin board display.

Bulletin Board Display
Use student clouds at the top of the bulletin board display to begin a large mural of optimism. Add a copy of "Friends" (page 12) and John Wesley's words (page 4) photocopied on decorative paper. Invite students to cut out and decorate large silhouettes of happy children. Add blank speech bubbles. Let groups work together to decide what to write in the speech bubbles. Add photographs of students participating in a project, helping each other. Have students make decorated banners to add to the display. They can use one of these phrases, or make up their own:

> *Optimists Care!*
> *Optimists Share!*
> *Optimists are Winners!*
> *Optimists are Good Friends!*
> *Optimists Succeed!*
> *Optimists Encourage One Another!*
> *Optimists Compliment One Another!*

Language Arts
- Invite students to write letters to their best friends. Have them tell what qualities they appreciate about their friends. Tie this in with a unit on the parts of a friendly letter and how to address an envelope.
- Provide books about the history of the Olympics and the events in the summer and winter games.

Music
- Challenge student groups to make up optimism songs, chants, cheers, jingles, or raps to perform for the class.
- Sing "If You're Happy and You Know It" with the class. Have students make up additional verses and sing them together. For example, *If you're happy and you know it, show you care . . . .*

Lesson 1

Discovering Extension Activities

Physical Education

Hold your own class Olympics by including physical events like the long jump, jumping rope, foot races, potato-sack races, and hopping races. Hold other events, like a spelling bee, math contest, art and poetry contests, or singing and dance contests.

Divide the class into committees to help plan the event:

- Events committee to determine which events to include
- Rules committee to determine rules for each event
- Scheduling committee to set up times for the events
- Awards committee to prepare ribbons or certificates
- Judging committee to select judges for various events
- Refreshment committee to provide and serve popcorn and juice, napkins, and paper plates
- Decorating committee to make decorations for the event
- Cleanup committee for after the Olympics

You could even have a committee to decide what committees you'll need. Encourage all students to join one committee. Invite students from other classes to participate in your Olympics. Encourage students to participate in at least two events.

Invite someone from a local newspaper to do a story about your class Olympics. Take pictures of the Olympic events and winners to make a class scrapbook.

Related Reading

The Berenstain Bears and the Trouble with Friends by Stan Berenstain (Random, 1987).

Friends by Helme Heine (Macmillan, 1982).

Hour of the Olympics by Mary Pope Osborne (Random, 1998).

Modern Olympic Superstars by George Sullivan (Putnam, 1979).

The Mud Flat Olympics by James Stevenson (Greenwillow, 1994).

Olympics by Dennis B. Fradin (Children's LB, 1983).

The Olympics by Peter Tatlow (Watts, 1988).

The 329th Friend by Marjorie Sharmat (Macmillan, 1979).

Communicating

Lesson 2

Materials

copy of "Silent Communication" (page 18), cut in half for each student pair

copy of "Shouting" (page 19) for each student pair

copy of "American Manual Alphabet" (page 21) for each student

copy of "Morse Code and Other Common Codes" (page 22) for each student

additional materials for selected activities

Insights: Words define ideas.
Words have power.
Power can be used for good or bad.
Words can be the sunshine of our days.
Words can become our worst nightmare.
Words can give us the courage we need—or lead to our defeat.
Words make the world easier to understand.

Objectives: Students will compare ways to communicate.
Students will discover the importance of good communication.

Total Time: Approximately 30–35 minutes
(Additional time may be needed depending on extension activities selected.)

Time	Activity	Procedure
5 minutes	Introduction	**Teacher:** What is communication? *Allow students to respond. Encourage them to mention that communication involves both talking and listening.* **Teacher:** How do people communicate with other people? *Allow students to respond: talking, books, movies, letters, newspapers, magazines, radio, telephones, computers, television, advertisements, music, dance, art.* **Teacher:** Does all communication require speaking? Is there a way to communicate with another person without saying a word or making any sounds? Today we will be experimenting with two ways to communicate. Let's see which method you like better.

© Fearon Teacher Aids FE11027   15

Lesson 2

Communicating

Time	Activity	Procedure
10 minutes	Silent Communication	*Divide students into pairs. Give each student one-half of the "Silent Communication" page. Have pairs sit face to face.* *Explain that one student will communicate a sentence to his or her partner without using any words or sounds. The other student must figure out the sentence. Have students take turns communicating each sentence without words.*
5 minutes	Anchoring	*Use the questions on the following page for group discussion.*
10 minutes	Shouting	*Divide the class into pairs. Give each student one half of the "Shouting" page.* *Tell students they will take turns reading the sentences out loud and deciding on the best answers. Have them circle their answers.* *Have students rejoin the group.*
10 minutes	Options	*Reread each scenario. Ask students which answer they selected and why. For each scenario, ask students for other positive ways to react to Pete.* **Teacher:** Why do you think people shout sometimes? Why do you think people use harsh words? How can we respond to people like Pete so we do not make the problem worse?

Communicating

Lesson 2

Time	Activity	Procedure
5 minutes	Anchoring	*Ask students to think about these two ways of communication: silent and shouting. Use the following questions for group discussion.* **Teacher:** Which way is easier, silent communication or shouting? Why? Which way gave you more problems? What were the problems? What words in the "Shouting" part of the activity were annoying? Why? Did your annoyance make you lose track of what was being said? Would it tempt you to say or do something you might not want to say or do? If someone shouts at you, would it be easy to misunderstand what the person really means? *Give students an example. Ask them if these two ways of saying something are the same. First, shout loudly, "Please put that away!" Then say the same words in a normal tone of voice.* **Teacher:** Even though my words were the same both times, how did my tone of voice change what you thought I meant?

Discussion Questions

1. How did you feel when you tried to communicate without words?
2. Was this way of communicating difficult? Why?
3. Did you have any trouble making yourself understood? (Ask for specific examples.)
4. Did you have any trouble understanding your partner? (Ask for specific examples.)
5. What are the advantages of communicating without words?

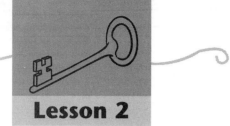

Lesson 2

Silent Communication

Student A

I walk.
I read.
I am hungry.
Please give me a book.
I have a dog.
This is good.

Student B

I talk.
Thank you.
I am thirsty.
Do you see the tree?
I am happy today.
This is not good.

Name _____

Lesson 2

Shouting

1. Pete comes up to you in class and shouts in a very loud, angry tone, "You're a loser!"

   What should you do?

   a. Scream at him and shout back, "You're a loser!"

   b. Scream and tell him to get lost.

   c. Change the topic and talk about something else.

2. Pete makes faces at you and screams, "You're a nerd!"

   What should you do?

   a. Make believe you didn't hear.

   b. Scream back, "Please stop!"

   c. Call him a bad name.

3. Pete yells loudly and angrily at you, "I hate you!"

   What should you do?

   a. Yell back and tell him to stop.

   b. Continue doing your work.

   c. Whisper something bad about Pete to your friend.

4. Pete says loudly, "I can stay up until midnight on Friday nights and you can't. You're a baby. Ha, ha!"

   What should you do?

   a. Ignore Pete completely and continue doing your work.

   b. Say, "I can, too," even though it isn't true.

   c. Tell everyone in the class that Pete was lying and he can't stay up until midnight either.

reproducible © Fearon Teacher Aids FE11027

Lesson 2

Communicating
Extension Activities

Language Arts
- Give each student a copy of the "American Manual Alphabet" to study. Help students learn to make the letters of the alphabet and spell words.
- Give each student a copy of "Morse Code and Other Common Codes." Invite students to use one of the codes to send and decipher messages.
- Write a short message on the chalkboard in Morse code, and have students decode it.

Library/Internet Search
Encourage students to search the library and Internet for books and information on Morse code, Braille, sign language, smoke signals, and other forms of codes. Have volunteers give reports on what they learned.

Social Studies
Invite someone who is hearing impaired or who teaches hearing impaired students to visit your classroom. Ask him or her to demonstrate sign language and teach the class to sign several words. This person could also demonstrate other skills people with hearing impairment can learn in order to improve communication. Have students prepare questions in advance and write them on index cards.

Related Reading
Anna's Silent World by Bernard Wolf (Harper, 1977).

Codes for Kids by Albert Burton (Whitman, 1976).

Communication by Aliki (Greenwillow, 1993).

The Conversation Club by Diane Stanley (Macmillan, 1983).

Dino the Deaf Dinosaur by Carole Addabbo (Hannacroix, 1998).

Expectations: A Gift for Blind Children by Douglas A. Menville (Braille Institute, 1996).

My First Book of Sign by Pamela Baker (Gallaudet, 1986).

Fun Time Codes and Mystery Messages by C. J. Verian (Children's Press, 1975).

Hand Signs: A Sign Language Alphabet by Kathleen Fain (Chronicle Books, 1995).

The Signed English Dictionary for Preschool and Elementary Levels by N. L. Lundborg (Gallaudet, 1980).

Name_____

American Manual Alphabet

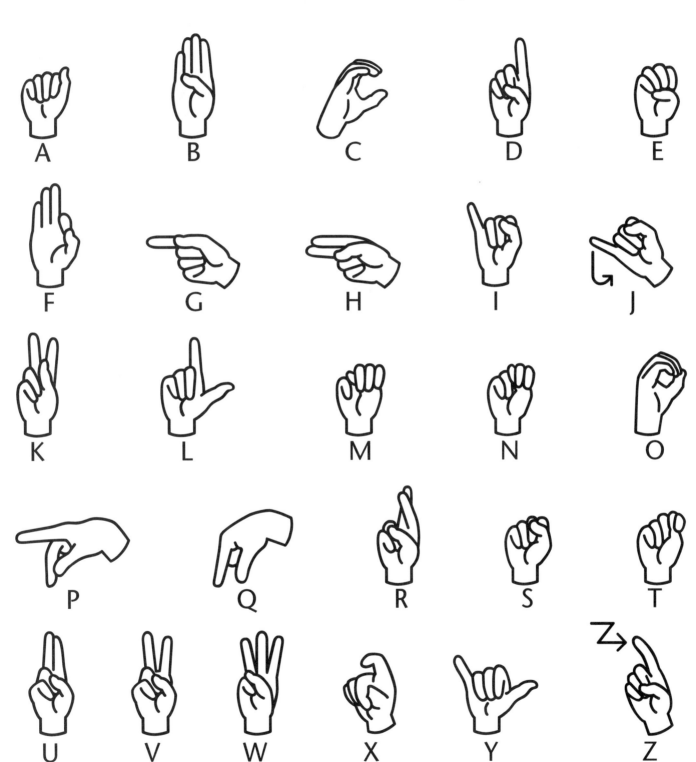

reproducible

Lesson 2

Name _____

Morse Code

A	●■
B	■●●●
C	■●■●
D	■●●
E	●
F	●●■●
G	■■●
H	●●●●
I	●●
J	●■■■
K	■●■
L	●■●●
M	■■
N	■●
O	■■■
P	●■■●
Q	■■●■
R	●■●
S	●●●
T	■
U	●●■
V	●●●■
W	●■■
X	■●●■
Y	■●■■
Z	■■●●

Other Common Codes

Many codes use numbers to stand for letters of the alphabet. The two most common use either forward or reverse numerical order.

A forward numerical code looks like this:

A = 1	**B** = 2	**C** = 3	**D** = 4
E = 5	**F** = 6	**G** = 7	**H** = 8
I = 9	**J** = 10	**K** = 11	**L** = 12
M = 13	**N** = 14	**O** = 15	**P** = 16
Q = 17	**R** = 18	**S** = 19	**T** = 20
U = 21	**V** = 22	**W** = 23	**X** = 24
Y = 25	**Z** = 26		

© Fearon Teacher Aids FE11027   reproducible

Success Words

Lesson 3

Materials

copy of "Cross Out the Negatives" (page 25) for each student

black markers or crayons

copy of "Success Words" (page 26) for each student

copy of "Phrases That Will Make You a Winner" (page 27) for each student

additional materials for selected activities

Insights: Words are powerful tools.
Words give us hope.
Words can motivate us.

Objective: Students will identify words that bring success.

Time: Approximately 30–40 minutes
(Additional time may be needed depending on extension activities selected.)

Time	Activity	Procedure
1 minutes	Introduction	**Teacher:** Let's brainstorm for a few minutes. Today we are looking for special words. I'll write the topics on the board and you see how many words you can name.
10 minutes	Brainstorm	*Write* Taste Words *on the chalkboard. List students' responses under the heading.* *Write* Smell Words. *List students' responses.* *Write* Sound Words. *List students' responses.* *Write* Sight Words. *List students' responses.* **Teacher:** How do these words give you a sensory feeling when you say them? What do these words do to make you more aware of your senses?

© Fearon Teacher Aids FE11027

23

Lesson 3

Success Words

Time	Activity	Procedure
10 minutes	Cross Out	Give each student a copy of "Cross Out the Negatives." Read each pair of words. Define any words that students may not understand. Have students cross out the negative word with a black marker or crayon. Continue through the list in the same manner. Periodically ask students to give examples of situations that further explain specific words.
5 minutes	Exploring	Give each student a copy of "Success Words." Read through the list. Talk about any words that might be new or unclear to students. Ask students to write their own success words at the bottom of the page. These can be favorite words from the list or students' own choices.
2 minutes	Anchoring	**Teacher:** Now that we learned so many positive words, why do you think these optimistic words are important? How will using these positive words make people around us feel good? Let's all make an effort to remember these optimistic words. Give each student a copy of "Phrases That Will Make You a Winner" to take home and share with their families. Invite them to ask family members for their favorite success words to add to the page.

Name _____

Lesson 3

Cross Out the Negatives

caring   uncaring
unfair   fair
sharing   selfish
mean   kind
polite   rude
doubting sure
grateful ungrateful
unfriendly friendly
false   honest
pleasant grumpy
unhappy   happy
just   unjust
stingy   generous
organized disorganized
sour   sweet
sincere   insincere
depressed cheerful
eager   reluctant
pessimistic optimistic
stupid   wise
capable   inept

reproducible   © Fearon Teacher Aids FE11027   25

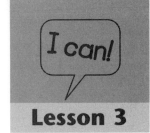

Lesson 3

Name _____

Success Words

acceptable
agree
appropriate

beautiful
blessed
bright
brilliant

caring
cheerful
chipper
confident
considerate
correct
courageous

dazzling
delightful

eager
elated
encouraging
energetic
enthusiastic

fair
fantastic
fascinating
friendly
funny

generous
glad
gleeful
good
gracious
grateful
great

happy
helpful

jolly
joyful
jubilant
just

kind

lovely
loving
lucky

merry

neat

optimistic

patient
pleasant
please
pleased
polite

radiant
responsible
rich

sharing
sincere
suitable
sunny

thank you

useful

Write your favorite words here: _____

_____

26   © Fearon Teacher Aids FE11027   reproducible

Name _____

Lesson 3

Phrases That Will Make You a Winner

Thank you
                I will plan
                          I will compliment
        I can
    I will care
                 I will try
                              I will share
        Please

Write your own success words:

1. _____

2. _____

3. _____

4. _____

Write words in the speech bubbles to show these two students using optimistic phrases.

reproducible   © Fearon Teacher Aids FE11027

Lesson 3

Success Words
Extension Activities

Art

- Have students cut various geometric shapes from colored construction paper. They can print one optimistic word in the center of each shape. Use the shapes as part of the bulletin board display to make a chain of success words.
- Spring is often thought of as a time for optimism. Have students design flowers that are "blooming" with positive words.

Bulletin Board Display

Cut large wave shapes from blue paper and place them along the bottom of the bulletin board. At the crest of each wave, have students add a success word. Add a copy of the "Success Words" page to the display. Use geometric shapes and name acrostic poems on the bulletin board.

Language Arts

- Have students use a thesaurus to find more success and optimistic words. Give students a copy of "Success Words." They can write name acrostic poems using words from this list as well as others that describe themselves. Show students this example:
- Students could also write name acrostic poems for their best friends. Have them add a decorative border to their poems and display them on the bulletin board.
- Write a group sequel to the story of Pete and Oliver. Have students sit in a circle. Start a new story about Pete and Oliver. Say the first sentence. Let students take turns adding one sentence until the story is complete. Tape-record or write the story as they tell it. Print the new story on chart paper and read it to the class the next day. Add stories to a class book of stories.
- Create word searches using five to ten success words. Do not include a list of hidden words. Have students search for the success words and write them on their papers when they find them.

P olite
A greeable
M erry
E ager
L aughing
A rtistic

© Fearon Teacher Aids FE11027

Success Words
Extension Activities

Lesson 3

Library/Internet Search
- Encourage students to find books or poems that include success words and share them with the class.

Math
- Have students take a poll among friends and family members. They can make a chart listing their ten favorite success words. Have them ask others which success words are their favorites. Make tally marks behind the words. After polling at least 15 to 20 people, have students add up the tally marks to see which success word most people liked best.
- Make a success-word graph. List ten success words in a column on chart paper. Divide the rest of the paper into small columns. Use at least 20 columns across. Each time you catch someone doing one of the actions listed, color in a box next to that word. At the end of a week, compare how often each action was demonstrated.

Social Studies
- Have students draw a map of their town or community. Let them rename the streets with optimistic names, like Lovely Lane and Sunny Street. Ask students if they think street names like this would make people happier.
- Have students make success-word signs for your classroom. Rename learning centers in your classroom using success words, e.g., Sunny Science Center or Radiant Reading Area. Have students work in teams to make and decorate signs for those areas.

Related Reading
1,400 Things for Kids to Be Happy About: The Happy Book by Barbara Ann Kipfer (Workman, 1994).

How Do I Feel? by Norma Simon (Whitman, 1979).

My Many Colored Day by Dr. Seuss (Knopf, 1996).

What Makes Me Happy? by C. Anholt (Candlewick, 1994).

Lesson 4

Probe-Em

Materials

copy of "Probe-Em Scenarios" (page 33)

copy of "Success Words" from Lesson 3 (page 26)

additional materials for selected activities

Insights: Problems provide a challenge.
Problems enable us to be detectives.
Facing and solving problems is a necessity of life. They make us stronger.
Problems are the spice of life. Without problems, life would be like mashed potatoes without butter, salt, or gravy.

Objectives: Students will explore scenarios depicting problems and the way others solved problems.
Students will use optimistic words to describe solutions and offer alternative solutions.

Time: Approximately 30–35 minutes
(Additional time may be needed depending on extension activities selected.)

Time	Activity	Procedure
5 minutes	Introduction	*Print the word PROBLEM on the board. Ask students the following questions, pausing to allow them to respond.* **Teacher:** What does the word *problem* mean? Do you have any problems? Would someone like to share one with us? How can we handle problems? What is the first thing you do when you discover you have a problem? *Try to elicit these responses:* *1. Define the problem.* *2. Investigate options.* *3. Make a plan.* *Under the word PROBLEM, write Probe-em.* *Ask students the following questions, pausing to allow them to respond.*

Probe-Em

Lesson 4

Time	Activity	Procedure
		Teacher: What does the word *probe* mean? Is there a way to probe into a problem? Can we probe into problems and find solutions? Let's find out! Let's probe-em.
20 minutes	Probe-em	*Display a copy of "Success Words" from Lesson 3.* *Read the "Probe-Em" scenarios, one at a time.* *Have students find the optimistic words on the "Success Words" page that they think best fills each blank. Discuss their word choices. If a student's answer differs from the suggested answer, ask the student to explain why he or she selected that option.* *For each scenario, be certain students understand the problem. Defining a problem is the first step to solving it.* *In many cases, there is more than one solution to a problem.* *In each scenario, one solution to the problem is given. Ask students to share ideas about other ways to solve the problem.*
5 minutes	Anchoring	*Ask students the following questions, pausing to allow them to respond.* **Teacher:** How do optimistic words and optimistic attitudes help solve problems? How does using success words in daily life help develop an optimistic attitude? Why aren't people optimistic all the time?

© Fearon Teacher Aids FE11027

Lesson 4

Probe-Em

Time	Activity	Procedure
	Anchoring (continued)	Can people be optimistic even when they have problems? How?
		If a problem seems too big for you to handle alone or you can't think of any way to solve the problem, what could you do?
		Encourage students to suggest that they can talk to others to help find a solution. Suggest various people for various types of problems, such as a doctor for a medical problem, and a parent, teacher, or school counselor for a personal problem.
		Reassure students that they can solve many problems alone and that there are people available to help solve big problems.

Name _____

Lesson 4

Probe-Em Scenarios

1. Marla saw her teacher picking up books that had fallen to the floor. Marla ran to help. Marla was _____. (helpful)

What was the problem? What did Marla do about it?

2. Kyla wanted to check something in the dictionary, but Jennie was using it. "May I borrow the dictionary for a minute, please?" she asked. Kyla was _____. (polite)

What was the problem? How did Kyla solve the problem?

3. Jordanna watched her friend search for crayons. Her friend's crayons were missing. Jordanna gave her crayon box to her friend to use. Jordanna was _____. (sharing)

What was the problem? Was it Jordanna's problem? What did she do about it?

4. Alex went to do his experiment at the science station, but it was a mess. The last person had not cleaned up the spilled water or thrown away the trash. Alex cleaned up the science station, did his experiment, and cleaned up his mess. Alex was _____. (neat, considerate, helpful)

What was the problem? What did Alex do about it?

5. Larry's great-grandmother lived alone in an apartment. Sometimes she was lonely. Larry liked to spend time with his great-grandmother and listen to her tell stories about the past. He ran many errands for her and helped her take out the trash. He was _____. (kind, helpful)

What was the problem? Was it Larry's problem? What did he do about it?

reproducible © Fearon Teacher Aids FE11027

Lesson 4

Probe-Em Extension Activities

Art
- Have students fold pieces of construction paper in half horizontally. Ask each student to draw a situation showing a problem on the front of his or her paper. Have them open the papers and draw solutions to the problems inside.
- Have students make totem poles using objects and optimist words that describe themselves. Let classmates guess the identity of the totem pole designers by reading the words and looking at the objects. (You may want to show students pictures of totem poles or model this activity first.)

Language Arts
- Have each student write an optimistic word, like *good,* then add other words that mean about the same (e.g., *obedient, considerate, kind, honest, just, dependable,* and so on) to make a word bank.
- Once they have word banks, have students incorporate their words into math poems. Write this sample on the board to help them get started:

    Two optimistic crows sat in a tree.
    One happy crow joined them.
    Then there were three.

Invite students to submit anonymous problems to you in writing. Read each problem to the class. Ask the class to brainstorm to help solve the problem.

Social Studies
- Give each student a U.S. or Canadian flag sticker. Have him or her place the sticker on white paper. Around the flag, ask students to write optimistic words they think about when they see the U.S. or Canadian flags.
- Have students think of a nickname for your city and your school that uses optimistic words, like the *School of Successful Students* or *Co-operative City*. Read the suggestions. Take a vote on which school and city nickname the class likes best.

Related Reading
The Book of Think, or, How to Solve a Problem Twice Your Size by Marilyn Burns (Little Brown, 1976).

I Can't Wait (A Children's Problem-Solving Book) by Elizabeth Crary (Parenting Press, 1996).

Let's Talk About Being Helpful by Joy Berry (Demco Media, 1996).

Mrs. Pollywog's Problem Solving Service by Ellen Javernick (Augsburg Fortress, 1995).

Believing Tower

Lesson 5

Materials

copy of "I Believe I Can" (page 37), photocopied on colorful paper for each student

large sheet of construction paper for each student

scissors

glitter pens

tape or glue

additional materials for selected activities

Insights: If we believe we can, we can.
Believing that you can do something is the first step to success.
Believing in yourself gives you an edge.
Believing you can succeed gives you a head start on succeeding.

Objectives: Students build self-confidence.

Time: Approximately 20 minutes
(Additional time may be needed depending on extension activities selected.)

Time	Activity	Procedure
5 minutes	Introduction	*Ask students the following questions, pausing to allow them to respond.* **Teacher:** How do you know if you can do something? Is there something inside your head that says, "I can!"? What's that feeling like? What words describe that feeling? Write *SELF-CONFIDENCE* on the board.
10 minutes	Create a Believing Tower	*Give each student a copy of the "I Believe I Can" page and a large sheet of construction paper, as well as glitter pens, scissors, and tape or glue.* *Read instructions for the "I Believe I Can" page with students and ask them to complete the activity with glitter pens.*

© Fearon Teacher Aids FE11027   35

Lesson 5

Believing Tower

Time	Activity	Procedure
	Create a Believing Tower (continued)	*Have students roll their construction papers into tube shapes and use tape or glue to hold them in place. The tubes can be short, fat, tall, or thin.* *Have students cut out the boxes from the completed "I Believe I Can" page. Glue or tape the "do" and "am" boxes to the top of the tower. Attach the "will" and "will be" boxes to the lower part of the tower.*
5 minutes	**Anchoring**	*Use the following questions for group discussion.*

Discussion Questions

1. How do you feel when you know you can do something?
2. How do you feel toward others when they are successful?
3. Look over all you can do on your tower. Doesn't it make you feel proud of your accomplishments?
4. Why is it important to review things we can do?
5. Does that make you feel good about yourselves?
6. Do you feel you want to accomplish more?
7. Would you feel more confident if you had more skills? Why?
8. One way to accomplish what you want to do is to make a plan. Does anyone have a plan they would like to share with the class?
9. Does being optimistic make learning new skills easier? How?
10. Is optimism an important part of the "I believe I can" attitude? Why?

© Fearon Teacher Aids FE11026

Name _____

Lesson 5

I Believe I Can

Read the words in each box. Write the word **do** on the line if this is something you can do now. Write the word **will** if it is something you will try to do in the future.

I _____ share.	I _____ say please.
I _____ listen.	I _____ say thank you.
I _____ help.	I _____ try new things.
I _____ compliment people.	I _____ accept compliments.
I _____ respect people.	I _____ be kind.

Read the words in each box. Write the word **am** if you can do it now. Write the words **will be** if you will try to do it in the future.

I _____ thoughtful.	I _____ organized.
I _____ optimistic.	I _____ confident.
I _____ polite.	I _____ generous.

Fill in the blanks with your own special skills.

_____ _____ _____	_____ _____ _____

reproducible   © Fearon Teacher Aids FE11027

Lesson 5

Believing Tower
Extension Activities

Art

- Have each student draw a picture of himself or herself that displays one of his or her "I can" or "I am" phrases.

- Hold a tower contest. Let students create three-dimensional towers using paper cylinders, cones, and cubes. Other tower entries could be made of blocks, empty thread spools, empty plastic bottles, and so on. Have students glue or tape the parts of the tower together for stability. They can add glitter, gold spray paint, lace, and other materials, for decorations. Invite another teacher to judge the contest. Have several categories such as tallest, shortest, most elaborate, and best decorated.

- Ask each student to bring in a cardboard box (shoe box, empty cracker or cereal box). Have students cover the boxes with construction paper and decorate them with paints or markers. Have them write their names on their boxes. Have students work together to assemble a class tower from the decorated boxes.

- Display the "Believing Towers" by hanging them from the ceiling with colored yarn or string. This can be done by taping the ends of the yarn or string to the top sides of the towers.

- Cut a stack of 4" (10-cm) squares from different-colored construction paper. When a student accomplishes a new goal, have him or her write it on a paper square *(I am patient. I can read all by myself).* Have the student sign his or her name. At the end of each day, students can attach their squares to the bulletin board to build a class "I can" tower.

Language Arts

- Have students start with words used in this lesson, such as *share, listen, help,* and *respect.* Have them add suffixes to those words to make new words such as *sharing* and *shared.*

- Have students write motivational letters to themselves. They should include today's date, three things they can do now, three things they hope to be able to do by the end of the year, and a plan of how they will accomplish this. Have students put the letters in envelopes, seal them, and write their names on the front. Collect the letters and save them. At the end of the year, return the letters and let students read what they wrote.

- Place students' names into a hat. Have each student draw a name and write a letter to that classmate, complimenting the person on his or her many accomplishments and encouraging the person to accomplish new goals. Students can look at that person's tower to learn about his or her accomplishments.

Believing Tower
Extension Activities

Lesson 5

Library/Internet Search
- Have students search the library and Internet for famous towers, such as the Eiffel Tower or Tower of Pisa. Have students research where the towers are located, and when and how they were built. Have them share their findings with the class.

Math
- Students can measure the towers' height and width and find which is the tallest, shortest, widest, narrowest. Have students work together to determine how tall a tower would be if they could stack all the towers on top of each other.
- Help students make a time line by year from birth to present. With a parent's help, fill in accomplishments for each year since birth.

Related Reading
I Can Do That: A Book About Confidence by Sally Schaedler (Time Life, 1997).

Flap Your Wings and Fly by Charlotte Pomerantz (Greenwillow, 1989).

The Little Engine That Could by Watty Piper (Scholastic, 1973).

The Little Red Ant and the Great Big Crumb: A Mexican Fable by Shirley Climo (Clarion, 1995).

Tower to the Sun by Colin Thompson (Knopf, 1997).

© Fearon Teacher Aids FE11027

Lesson 6

On Your Mark, Get Set, Plan!

Materials

one sheet of lined paper for each student

pencils

additional materials for selected activities

Insights: Plans prepare you for giant leaps.
Plans let you take charge of your life.
You are in control when you make plans for yourself.
Without a plan, you will accomplish little.

Objective: Students will understand how planning can help them organize their lives.

Time: Approximately 20 minutes
(Additional time may be needed depending on extension activities selected.)

Time	Activity	Procedure
5 minutes	Introduction	**Teacher:** Let's pretend we're going on vacation. What do we need to do to get ready? *Allow students to respond:* Plan when and where to go. Plan how to get there. Plan what to take. Plan what to do there. Plan how to take care of things (pets, mail, and so on) while you're gone. *Ask students the following questions, pausing to allow them to respond.* **Teacher:** Taking a trip involves making many plans. When you make a plan, does it help to write it down? Why? Can anyone make a plan for every event? Why not? Once a plan is made, can it ever be changed? Why or why not? Can you give me an example of when a plan might need to be changed?

40 © Fearon Teacher Aids FE11027

On Your Mark, Get Set, Plan!

Lesson 6

Time	Activity	Procedure
	Introduction (continued)	What would happen if someone tried to build a house without a plan? What would happen if teachers didn't make lesson plans? What would happen if an airline pilot didn't make a plan for where the plane was going? Can students make a plan to improve a school skill like writing? Let's find out.

15 minutes	**Following a Plan**	We can all improve how neatly we write our names. To do that, we should follow a plan.
		
		Write the following on the board:
		My plan is to improve writing my name by working on . . .
		    . . . the letter size
		    . . . the letter shapes
		    . . . the slant
		    . . . staying on the baseline
		    . . . neatness
		
		Review the plan with the class. Then hand out ruled paper and pencils.
		
		Teacher: Is everyone ready to begin?
		
		Please write your name neatly on the first line.
		
		Look at the steps to the plan. Then write your name again four more times. Try to do better each time.
		
		While students are writing, walk around the classroom offering praise for those who are doing well and trying hard. Point out any improvement you notice as they write.
		
		When students finish, ask them to share their writing with a partner.

© Fearon Teacher Aids FE11027   41

Lesson 6

On Your Mark, Get Set, Plan!

Time	Activity	Procedure
5 minutes	Anchoring	Ask students the following questions, pausing to allow them to respond. **Teacher:** Did having a plan to improve your writing help? Why or why not? Did each point in the plan help keep you on target? Why or why not? How could our plan be better? If we made a plan for another skill, do you think it would help to break the plan down into specific tasks? Let's make another plan for improving a skill together. For what skill should we make a plan? *Write one suggestion on the board:* Our plan to . . . What will we need to do? *Write all suggestions under the first sentence. If the plan needs steps that must be done in a specific order, have students determine which should be done first, second, third, and so on. Number each step in the plan.* *If it's feasible, implement the plan in your classroom, either immediately or in the near future.* **Teacher:** What other things could we make plans for? Do you think making a plan helps? If making a plan helps, then it's a good idea to make plans. On your mark, get set, plan!

On Your Mark, Get Set, Plan!
Extension Activities

Lesson 6

Art

- Have students accordion-fold a 6-inch (15-cm) strip of construction paper. At the top, have them write their names. On each fold, ask them to write a skill they would like to improve or acquire. Hang the complete lists of goals on the bulletin board.

- Have each student cut a large triangle from construction paper. At the top, have students write one of their goals. Ask students to make plans to achieve these goals and write the steps of their plans inside the triangles. They can divide triangles into smaller triangles and write one step in each section. Remind them that they should have a plan in mind as to how they will design their triangle plans.

- Periodically review the plans with students and discuss progress toward the goals. Help students revise their plans as needed.

Bulletin Board Display

- Find a picture of an elaborate house. Do not show the picture to the class. Draw one feature of the house—perhaps the roof or a door. Pass the page to a student and ask him or her to add another feature. Let each student add something to the house picture. When they finish, compare the final drawing to the original picture. Is it anything like the original? Probably not, and that is what can happen without a plan.

- Draw a floor plan of your classroom to scale. Put in only the dimensions, doors, windows, blackboards, and other items that cannot be moved. Have students work in pairs. Give each pair a copy of the floor plan. Ask them to redesign your classroom using their best ideas. Display the finished drawings. If any are feasible, implement them.

- Make a bulletin board called *Plan It!* Display students' goal lists, triangle plans, and the original house and finished house drawing, and classroom floor plans.

Related Reading

Every Kid's Guide to Decision Making and Problem Solving by Joy Berry (Children's Press, 1987).

From Blueprint to House by Franz Hogner (Carolrhoda, 1986).

Jackson's Plan by Linda Tally (Marsh Media, 1998).

Sarah's Secret Plan by Linda Johns (Troll, 1995).

Lesson 7

Smiles and Giggles

Materials

copy of "Smiles and Giggles" (page 47)

one sheet of lined paper for each student

colored construction paper

pencils

markers

additional materials for selected activities

Insights: Humor chases fears away.
Laughing helps conquer anxiety.
Smiles and giggles put the body in an optimistic mood.
A laugh a day keeps the doctor away.

Objective: Students will learn how humor helps dispel anxiety and promotes optimism.

Time: Approximately 30–40 minutes
(Additional time may be needed depending on extension activities selected.)

Time	Activity	Procedure
5 minutes	Introduction	**Teacher:** What would happen if your cat started laughing? (Pause.) She'd be a gigglepuss! Who knows a good funny joke? Will you share it with the class? *Select several students to tell jokes. If any student tells an "off-color" or put-down joke, be certain to let the class know how you feel about that without causing embarrassment to the student. Prepare the class in advance by setting guidelines for jokes if you feel it is necessary.* *When students are all laughing from good jokes, continue with the following questions. Pause to allow students to respond.* **Teacher:** How does laughing make you feel? What happens when you laugh?

© Fearon Teacher Aids FE11027

Smiles and Giggles

Lesson 7

Time	Activity	Procedure
	Introduction (continued)	Does laughing help you forget your problems? Does laughing help you feel better?
5 minutes	Smiles	*Read jokes from the "Smiles, Giggles, and Jokes" page. Allow students time to laugh and talk about these jokes.* *Give each student lined paper and a pencil. Tell them they will be working on a draft copy now, so not to worry about erasing or crossing out.*

15-20 minutes	Personal Smiles and Giggles	**Teacher:** Now to work. Your first smiles and giggles assignment is to write a four-lined poem using your name and words that rhyme.
		
		Start the first sentence with:
		   My name is . . . and write your first name.
		
		When students are ready to continue, tell them that they should add three more lines to their poems. Write this example on the board and read it to the class:
		
		   My name is Paul.
		   I am tall.
		   I won't fall
		   If you call.
		
		When students finish, ask volunteers to share their poems with the class.
		
		Teacher: Our next smiles and giggles activity will be to write a tongue twister using your name. Who knows what a tongue twister is?
		
		Allow students to respond.
		
		Teacher: Right, a tongue twister is a sentence with many words that start with the same sound. Let's try this one together.

© Fearon Teacher Aids FE11027

Lesson 7

Smiles and Giggles

Time	Activity	Procedure
	Personal Smiles and Giggles (continued)	*Write on the board:* Tim twisted his tongue ten times. *Say this tongue twister together several times.* **Teacher:** Now it's your turn to write a tongue twister using your first name. *Again, let volunteers share their tongue twisters with the class. Many of these will be funny.*
5 minutes	Anchoring	**Teacher:** How did writing and listening to the silly poems and tongue twisters make you feel? Does humor make you feel more optimistic? How? Why do you think many adults like to read the comics in the newspaper? Do you think it helps people be more optimistic if they start their day with smiles and giggles? **Note:** *After this lesson, help students polish their poems and tongue twisters, correcting grammar and spelling errors. Have students rewrite their poems and tongue twisters on colored construction paper with colored markers. They can add borders and designs. Display the finished poems and tongue twisters for all to enjoy.*

Name _____

Smiles, Giggles, and Jokes  Lesson 7

Knock, knock.
Who's there?
Justin.
Justin who?
Justin time for dinner.

Knock, knock.
Who's there?
Detail.
Detail who?
Detail of the cat is in back.

Knock, knock.
Who's there?
Wayne.
Wayne who?
**Wayne, Wayne, go away.
Come again another day.**

Knock, knock.
Who's there?
Canoe.
Canoe who?
Canoe come over
and play?

Knock, knock.
Who's there?
Irish.
Irish who?
Irish I had a million dollars.

Knock, knock.
Who's there?
Carl.
Carl who?
Carl get you there faster
than a bike.

Knock, knock.
Who's there?
Boo.
Boo who?
Don't cry, it's only me.

Knock, knock.
Who's there?
Amos.
Amos who?
A mosquito.

Knock, knock.
Who's there?
Dog.
Dog who?
Dogs don't who, owls do.

Knock, knock.
Who's there?
Hatch.
Hatch who?
Bless you.

Knock, knock.
Who's there?
Howl.
Howl who?
**Howl it be if I come to
your house tomorrow?**

Knock, knock.
Who's there?
A cheetah.
A cheetah who?
A cheetah never wins.

**Do you know the quickest
way to get home?**
Run!

What are the largest ants?
Eleph*ants*

**Where do you take a sick
dog?**
To the *dog*tor.

**Why did the baker stop
making doughnuts?**
He got tired of the *hole*
business.

**How do you pet a
porcupine?**
Very carefully.

reproducible © Fearon Teacher Aids FE11027

Lesson 7

Smiles and Giggles
Extension Activities

Art
Let students draw their favorite cartoon characters, then make up a rhyme or alliteration using the characters' names.

Language Arts
- Make a class joke book. Ask students to write their favorite jokes, illustrate them, and place them in a three-ring binder for everyone to enjoy. Encourage students to add their tongue twisters, favorite puns, and riddles.
- Have students make up "stinky pinky" jokes. A stinky pinky is a joke with a two- or three-word rhyming answer.

   Examples:
   What do you call a plump feline?
   (A fat cat)

   Where do nachos swim?
   (In chip dip)

   What do you call a five-cent cucumber?
   (A nickel pickle)

   What do you call a robin that needs a bath?
   (A dirty birdie)

Library/Internet Search
Have students search the library and Internet for good jokes. There are many Internet sites devoted to children's jokes, riddles, and puns.

Related Reading
ABC Animal Riddles by Susan Joyce (Peel Productions, 1999).

Beastly Riddles: Fishy, Flighty and Buggy, Too by Joseph Low (Macmillan, 1983).

The Carsick Zebra and Other Animal Riddles by David Adler (Bantam, 1983).

Elephants Never Forget! A Book of Elephant Jokes by Diane Burns (Lerner, 1987).

Mik Brown's Riddle Book by Mik Brown (Watts, 1988).

A Pack of Riddles by William R. Gerler (Dutton, 1975).

A Positive Attitude Is Contagious

Lesson 8

Materials

copy of "Do I Have a Positive Attitude?" (page 51) for each student

pencils

additional materials for selected activities

Insights: Your optimism shapes your attitude.
A positive attitude is your greatest asset.
A positive attitude gives you a head start.

Objective: Students will examine how their attitudes affect them.

Time: Approximately 25 minutes
(Additional time may be needed depending on extension activities selected.)

Time	Activity	Procedure
5 minutes	Introduction	**Teacher:** Have you ever gotten up in the morning and known something good was going to happen? How does that make you feel? *Ask students to stand and jump up and down. Comment on the expressions on their faces. They will probably mostly be smiling.* *Now ask students to put on angry faces and jump up and down.* *Ask students the following questions, pausing to allow them to respond.* **Teacher:** Is it possible to be angry when you jump up and down? Do you think certain activities can change the way you feel? Did you know that your attitude can change things? Can you give me examples?

© Fearon Teacher Aids FE11027

49

Lesson 8

A Positive Attitude Is Contagious

Time	Activity	Procedure
15 minutes	Exploring Attitude	Give each student a copy of "Do I Have a Positive Attitude?" and a pencil. Read each statement out loud. Have students circle *happy* or *not happy*. When they finish, ask students to count the number of times they circled *happy* and write the number on the total line. Have them do the same for *not happy*.
2 minutes	Anchoring	**Teacher:** Did this little quiz tell you anything about yourself? Did you discover anything about yourself that you want to work on? If you circled more *happy*s, you have an optimistic, positive attitude. Keep up the good work! If you circled more *not happy*s, you can try to be more positive about yourself when you do good things or when good things are said and done to you. Remember, you are in control!

Name _____

Lesson 8

Do I Have a Positive Attitude?

When I tell a joke I feel . . .	happy	not happy
When I listen to a joke I feel . . .	happy	not happy
When I help someone I feel . . .	happy	not happy
When someone helps me I feel . . .	happy	not happy
When I say thank you I feel . . .	happy	not happy
When someone says thank you I feel . . .	happy	not happy
When I share with someone I feel . . .	happy	not happy
When someone shares with me I feel . . .	happy	not happy
When I compliment someone I feel . . .	happy	not happy
When someone compliments me I feel . . .	happy	not happy
When I make a plan for something I feel . . .	happy	not happy
When I do my work well I feel . . .	happy	not happy
When I practice and learn a skill I feel . . .	happy	not happy
When I have a positive attitude I feel . . .	happy	not happy
TOTAL:	_____	_____

reproducible © Fearon Teacher Aids FE11027

51

Lesson 8

A Positive Attitude Is Contagious
Extension Activities

Art
- Students can draw pictures of themselves doing things that make them happy. Ask them to write sentences on the back of the pictures describing why these activities make them happy.
- Using old magazines, have students cut out positive words and pictures of people acting in positive ways. Let them cover one section of a bulletin board with the pictures to make a class collage.

Language Arts
- One way to help students develop positive attitudes is to let them imagine they are superheroes. Read several tall tales to the class to get them into the spirit. Stories of Paul Bunyan and Babe the Blue Ox are perennial favorites. After listening to several tall tales, have students write their own tall tales with themselves as the heroes. Read some of the stories to the class. Ask students to talk about how picturing themselves as superheroes can help build positive attitudes.
- Have students work in pairs to write motivational, optimistic slogans that could be used as bumper stickers. Have them neatly print their slogans with colored markers on construction paper. Display the bumper stickers on your classroom door and walls.
- Encourage students to write something positive about themselves in their journals every day. Have them add a statement about what they most want to work on—a skill they wish to learn or something they wish to change about themselves. Have students develop plans to accomplish these goals.

Related Reading
Crossing the New Bridge by E. McCully (Putnam, 1994).

Good Times on Grandfather Mountain by Jacqueline Martin (Orchard, 1997).

Pecos Bill by Dewey Ariane (Greenwillow, 1983).

Paul Bunyan: A Tall Tale by Steven Kellogg (Morrow, 1984).

Paul Bunyan and Babe the Blue Ox by Jan Gleiter and Kathleen Thompson (Raintree, 1985).

The Singing Hill by Meindert DeJong (Harper, 1962).

Rainbow Optimism

Lesson 9

Materials

white construction paper for each student

crayons or markers

additional materials for selected activities

Insights: Rainbows are nature's wake-up call.
Rainbows stretch across the sky to show how far we can go if we try.
Rainbows follow a storm to give us hope.

Objective: Students will relate the colors of the rainbow to optimism.

Time: Approximately 30–45 minutes
(Additional time may be needed depending on extension activities selected.)

Time	Activity	Procedure
5 minutes	Introduction	*Ask students the following questions. Pause for responses.* **Teacher:** Do colors ever affect you? How? Which colors make you happy? Are there colors that make you feel brave? Which ones? Are there colors that make you feel more energetic? Which ones? Are there colors that make you feel hopeful? Which ones? Are these colors part of the rainbow? Can colors show us the optimistic way? Let's find out.
10 minutes	Rainbow Optimism Activity	*Write the following on the board:* **R O Y G B I V** *Explain that these letters stand for the colors of the rainbow, in order: red, orange, yellow, green, blue, indigo, violet.*

© Fearon Teacher Aids FE11027

53

Rainbow Optimism

Lesson 9

Time	Activity	Procedure
	Rainbow Optimism Activity (continued)	Have students draw rainbows with wide bands of color using crayons or markers on white paper. They can follow the letter order to get the colors in the right order. Have them blend together the areas where two colors meet. **Teacher:** Earlier we talked about how some colors make us feel. Now let's think of rainbow words. We are going to brainstorm for positive words for each color of the rainbow. Write the names of the seven colors on the board. As students name colors and words, write the words under the color names. Some words may be listed under more than one color. When the list is completed, ask students to pick their favorite word for each color. Have them write those words in fancy letters across the bands of their rainbows.
10 minutes	Anchoring	Use these questions. Pause for responses. **Teacher:** Does having your favorite colors around you make you feel happy? Do you feel happy when you wear clothes in your favorite colors? How can these colors and words help you feel more optimistic? Can you feel happy just by thinking of these colors? Use students' optimism rainbow drawings as part of a colorful bulletin board display.

© Fearon Teacher Aids FE11027

Rainbow Optimism
Extension Activities

Lesson 9

Art
Ask a local paint store for cards showing paint samples in a variety of colors. Let students cut the samples apart and use them to make mosaics of rainbows or other objects.

Just for Fun
- Ask students to wear clothing of their favorite color on a specified day. This would work well on the day you plan to use this lesson. Have each student bring in one item in his or her favorite color. Ask students to share with others why they chose specific colors as their favorites.
- Each day for a week, announce the "Color of the Day" for the next day. Ask everyone to wear as much of that color as they can. Tie in at least one activity each day with the color of the day.

Language Arts
Ask students to imagine what that might find if they could travel to the end of a rainbow. Have them write short stories telling what they found at the end of the rainbow. Invite them to illustrate their tales as well.

Math
Have students predict which colors they think most of their classmates like best and least. Then take two surveys to find out. List colors (primary and secondary) in a column on chart paper. Divide the rest of the paper into small columns. Have students color in a box next to their favorite color on one sheet and next to their least favorite color on the other. If you turn the chart paper sideways when you finish, you will have a bar graph.

Music
Sing this song with your class to the tune of "Row, Row, Row Your Boat."

Paint, paint,
I like to paint,
I paint with red and blue.
I like pink and violet
And sometimes purple, too.

Have students make up songs about colors and sing them to familiar melodies. They can add percussion instruments, other sound effects, and motions to the songs, then perform them for the class.

© Fearon Teacher Aids FE11027

Lesson 9

Rainbow Optimism
Extension Activities

Science

- Explore a color wheel. Let students experiment with combining different colors of poster paints or watercolors. Explore primary and secondary colors. Encourage them to find out what happens when they mix blue and yellow or red and yellow. Have them record the colors they mixed and the colors that resulted.

- Have each student set up his or her own survey and a chart to record responses. At the top of the page, students should write a question that summarizes the survey (for example, *What is your favorite day of the week?*). The options for answers (*Monday, Tuesday,* and so on) can be written in a column on the left side of the page. When students finish their surveys, have them report their results to the class.

- Take a class survey. *How many are wearing red today? How many are wearing blue? Which color is predominant?* Try this on different days of the week, and have students compare the results.

Writing

Read several *Just So* stories by Rudyard Kipling or other fables that explain why something in nature became the way it is. Have students write their own stories about how the rainbow got its colors.

Related Reading

The Beginning of the Armadillos by Rudyard Kipling (Bedrick, 1983).

>Other books in this series include *The Butterfly That Stamped, The Cat That Walked by Himself,* and *The Crab That Played by the Sea*. Many other versions of single stories from the *Just So* stories, illustrated by different artists, are available.

Chasing Rainbows by Charlotte Allen (Severn House, 1992).

Color from Rainbow to Laser by Franklyn Branley (Cromwell, 1978).

Colors by Gallimard Jeunesse and Pascale de Bourgoing (Scholastic, 1991).

Green Is Beautiful by Margaret Rogers (Rourke, 1982).

A Rainbow of My Own by Don Freeman (Viking, 1966).

Rainbows and Ice Cream by C. Elbert (Iowa Library, 1983).

Unseen Rainbows, Silent Songs, the World Beyond Your Senses by S. Goodman (Athenium, 1995).

Smiles Are Contagious

Lesson 10

Materials

lined paper

construction paper

glitter pens, crayons, or markers

pencils

copy of "The Case of the Missing Smile" (page 60) for each student

additional materials for selected activities

Insights: Smile, and the whole world smiles with you.
A smile can carry you through many difficulties.
A smile can make a cloudy day seem bright and sunny.

Objective: Students will explore the power of a smile.

Time: Approximately 25 minutes
(Additional time may be needed depending on extension activities selected.)

Time	Activity	Procedure
5 minutes	Introduction	**Teacher:** Have you ever caught a cold? Having a cold isn't any fun. Colds are contagious. You can catch one if you're around someone who has a cold. Are yawns contagious? *Try a huge yawn. See how many students yawn, too. This should make your point.* **Teacher:** How about smiles? Are smiles contagious? *Share a big smile with the class and most will smile back.* **Teacher:** How do you feel when someone smiles at you? How can we share our smiles with others? Smiles are one way of sharing your optimistic attitude with others. What are other ways we can share our good feelings with others?

© Fearon Teacher Aids FE11027   **57**

Lesson 10

Smiles Are Contagious

Time	Activity	Procedure
	Introduction (continued)	*Some ideas for sharing an optimistic attitude: telling a joke; singing a happy song; giving someone special a hug; making someone a present; calling someone on the phone; sending a letter or card to someone far away; visiting; sharing a cartoon, funny story, or funny poem, and so on.*
15 minutes	Happy Cards	**Teacher:** One way to share a smile with a friend is to send a cheerful card. Today we are going to make happy cards. *Give students construction paper and glitter pens, crayons, or markers. Show them three ways to fold the construction paper to make a greeting card: in half vertically, in half horizontally, or in quarters.* *Ask students to make cards for friends or family members. They should decorate the cards with happy pictures, write cheerful words or a happy poem on the cards, and sign their names.*
5 minutes	Anchoring	*Give each student a sheet of lined paper and pencil.* **Teacher:** Sending a happy card is only one way to share a smile. Let's all decide on two other ways we can share a smile with someone today. Write two ways you will share a smile with someone today. Remember, you can share a smile with a million people and still have a whole smile left.

© Fearon Teacher Aids FE11027

Smiles Are Contagious
Extension Activities

Lesson 10

Art
- Give each student a copy of the poem "The Case of the Missing Smile." Read the poem aloud together. Ask students to copy the poem onto a sheet of drawing paper, then draw five pictures on the page, one for each verse of the poem.
- Have students work in pairs to paint big, cheerful flowers on large pieces of paper or posterboard. Ask them to write a saying that will make others smile when they read it and see the picture. Display the posters in the hall near your classroom.

Language Arts
- Tell students their best friends lost their smiles and can't seem to find them anywhere. What can they do? Ask each student to write a short story or poem about what happened to his or her friend's smile and how the student helped put it back in place.
- Ask students to write bright, happy poems—ones that will bring smiles to people's faces, or silly ditties that will make people giggle. Add silly illustrations. Display the poems for all to enjoy.
- Provide students with books of limericks and silly poems. Ogden Nash and Edward Lear are always fun. Have students share their favorite limericks or silly verses with the class.
- Play this game with the class to see how long someone can keep from smiling. Students take turns standing in front of the class without smiling. The other students must try to make that person smile by smiling and making silly faces. They could take turns telling funny jokes or singing silly songs. Whatever it takes. Hopefully, no one will be able to resist for more than a minute or two.

Related Reading
Can You Help Me Find My Smile? by Carl Sommer (Advance Publications, 1997).
Daffy Down Dillies: Silly Limericks by Edward Lear (Boyds Mills Press, 1992).
The Magical Moonball by Laura L. Seeley (Peachtree, 1992).
Smile If You're Human by Neal Layten (Dial, 1999).

Lesson 10

Name _____

The Case of the Missing Smile

I lost my smile, I don't know where.
Did I leave it behind Dad's chair?
I looked under the rug, but it wasn't there.
Maybe it was eaten by a polar bear.

I climbed a tree. I looked far and wide
Where, oh where, could a smile hide?
I had one this morning, it was big and wide.
Maybe I left it in the garden outside.

I checked in the closet and under my bed.
I found some dust balls and an old rusty sled.
Maybe I left it in the book I read
Or put it in the sandwich I made with rye bread.

Where it went is a mystery.
If you should find it, will you send it to me?
Oh, wait a minute, I think I see
That smile I thought was lost from me.

I looked in the mirror and what did I see?
My very own smile, smiling back at me.
Now it's no longer a mystery
My smile is back where it should be.

—*Cindy Barden*

The Optimists Club

Lesson 11

Materials

copy of "Optimists Club Pledge" (page 63) for each student

copy of "Optimists Club Membership Certificate" (page 64) for each student, filled out in advance

glitter pens (to sign certificates)

Insights: Optimist words form attitudes;
Attitudes shape beliefs;
Beliefs govern motivation;
Motivation brings success.

Objective: Students will determine eligibility for the Optimists Club.

Time: Approximately 30 minutes

Time	Activity	Procedure
5 minutes	Introduction	*Ask students the following questions, pausing to allow students to respond.* **Teacher:** Has anyone ever belonged to a club? Which one? How did belonging to the club make you feel? What did you have to do to join the club? What keeps a club together? What keeps friendships together? Is there a relationship between friendship and belonging to a club? Today we are going to form our own class club. It will be called the *Optimists Club*. Why do you think that is a good name for our club? What are some things we need to do to form a club? *Encourage the response that the club needs to have rules.*

© Fearon Teacher Aids FE11027

Lesson 11

The Optimists Club

Time	Activity	Procedure
	Introduction (continued)	If it's an optimists club, what types of rules should we have? *Write students' suggestions on the board. Be sure to highlight the main points of the pledge.*
5 minutes	Making a Pledge	**Teacher:** Do you know what a pledge is? A pledge is a promise to do something. When people join a club, they usually make a pledge. We have a pledge for our club, too. *Hand out the completed pledges and certificates.* *Read the pledge, line by line. Ask students to repeat the words after you. When they finish, ask them to sign the pledges. Display their pledges on the bulletin board.* *After a week or so, send the pledges and certificates home for students to share with their families.*

© Fearon Teacher Aids FE11027

Name _____

Lesson 11

Optimists Club Pledge

I will try . . .

to be positive in my words and actions.

to maintain a positive attitude.

to believe in myself.

to share with others.

to care for others.

to help others.

to try new things enthusiastically.

to give compliments.

to respect others.

to set goals and make plans.

I will be the best optimist I can be!

Signed: _____

Certificate of Membership
Optimists Club

_____

is an outstanding member of the Optimists Club!

Teacher's Signature_____

Date _____